# THE HOW AND WHY WONDER® BOOK OF

# PREHISTORIC
# MAMMALS

Written by MARTIN L. KEEN
Illustrated by JOHN HULL
Editorial Production: DONALD D. WOLF

Edited under the supervision of
   Dr. Paul E. Blackwood,  Washington, D. C.

Text and illustrations approved by
   Oakes A. White, Brooklyn Children's Museum, Brooklyn, New York

✕ ALLAN PUBLISHERS, INC.
Exclusive Distributors

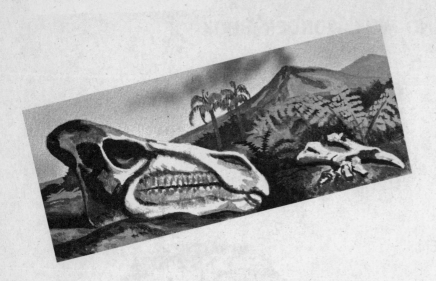

# Introduction

*The How and Why Wonder® Book of Prehistoric Mammals* takes its reader on a guided tour into the past far beyond the time when men appeared upon the earth. The purpose of this tour is to glimpse the variety of mammals that have walked upon the land or, in some cases, swum the seas. Mammals are warm-blooded animals whose babies are born alive and live on their mother's milk. Many mammals, including man, are on the earth today. This book, however, deals primarily with mammals that no longer live upon the earth.

Since these mammals are no longer alive, scientists learn about them mainly by studying their fossil remains, which are still to be found in the rocks of the earth. Scientists who specialize in reading this record of past life in the rocks are called *paleontologists*. This book suggests the exciting work they do in reconstructing the appearance and habits of mammals from a few fossil bones, in giving a date to their time on earth, and in relating mammals to other animals that came before them and after them in the long story of life.

In this book, the story of mammals is placed within the sweep of the longer stories of our changing earth's surface and of other forms of animal life. It may be read as an intriguing guide book to a tour through time and also used in the home and school library as a reference work on prehistoric mammals.

*Paul E. Blackwood*

Dr. Blackwood is a professional employee in the U. S. Office of Education. This book was edited by him in his private capacity and no official support or endorsement by the Office of Education is intended or should be inferred.

# Contents

ALTICAMELUS

CENOZOIC ERA
60 MILLION YEARS

CENOZOIC PERIOD

PLEISTOCENE EPOCH
PLIOCENE EPOCH
MIOCENE EPOCH
OLIGOCENE EPOCH
EOCENE EPOCH
PALEOCENE EPOCH

1-60 MILLION YEARS AGO

MAN
AGE OF MAMMALS

MASTODON
EOHIPPUS
MEGATHERIUM

MESOZOIC ERA
120 MILLION YEARS

CRETACEOUS
PERIOD

130 MILLION YEARS AGO

JURASSIC PERIOD

155 MILLION YEARS AGO

TRIASSIC PERIOD

185 MILLION YEARS AGO

AGE OF REPTILES
AGE OF REPTILES

MIXOSAURUS
TYRANNOSAURUS

PALEOZOIC ERA    335 MILLION YEARS

PERMIAN PERIOD

210 MILLION YEARS AGO

CARBONIFEROUS
PERIOD

265 MILLION YEARS AGO

DEVONIAN
PERIOD

320 MILLION YEARS AGO

AGE OF REPTILES
COAL AGE
AGE OF FISH

DIMETRODON
EUSTHENOPTERON
SALTOPOSUCHUS

SILURIAN PERIOD

360 MILLION YEARS AGO

ORDOVICIAN
PERIOD

440 MILLION YEARS AGO

CAMBRIAN PERIOD

520 MILLION YEARS AGO

AGE OF INVERTEBRATES

PLACODERM
EURYPTERID
LAMP SHELL
CORAL

CRYPTOZOIC EON
ABOUT 4½ BILLION YEARS

PRE-CAMBRIAN ERA

600 MILLION YEARS AGO

4-5 BILLION YEARS AGO
4½ BILLION YEARS AGO
5 BILLION YEARS AGO

AGE OF HIDDEN LIFE

NO LIVING THINGS
DEEP PART OF EARTH'S CRUST FORMED
APPROXIMATE BEGINNING OF EARTH AS PLANET

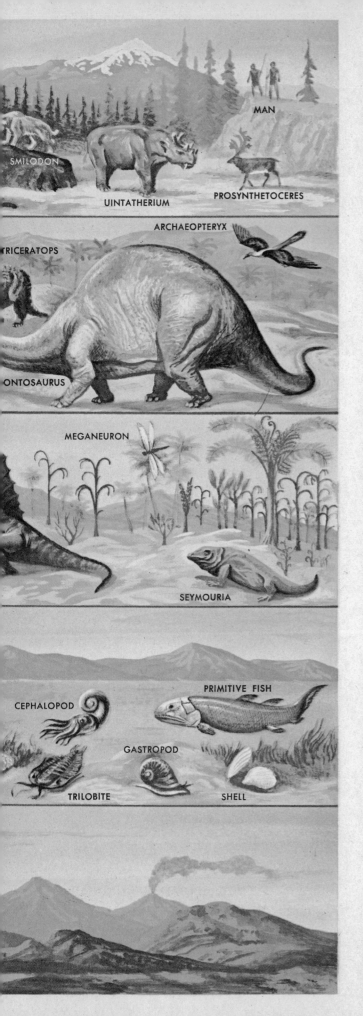

SMILODON

MAN

UINTATHERIUM

PROSYNTHETOCERES

ARCHAEOPTERYX

TRICERATOPS

ONTOSAURUS

MEGANEURON

SEYMOURIA

CEPHALOPOD

PRIMITIVE FISH

GASTROPOD

TRILOBITE

SHELL

# The Record of Past Life

When Vice-President-elect Thomas Jefferson arrived in the nation's capital, Philadelphia, in 1797, he brought with him a box from his home at Monticello. The box contained many large bones and claws that had been found on the floor of a cave in western Virginia. Two years later, Jefferson delivered an address to the American Philosophical Society, describing the animal from which he believed the large bones and claws had come. He called the animal Megalonyx, or "great claw." He believed the Megalonyx to be a gigantic lion, and he thought that some of these lions might yet be roaming the great forests of the American West and Northwest.

We know, today, that the bones Jefferson studied were really those of a huge ground sloth that lived millions of years ago in what is now North America. Scientists call this sloth *Megalonyx Jeffersoni* in honor of the discoverer of its bones. The Megalonyx was a huge, hairy animal that walked on the sides of its four long-clawed feet, as today's sloths do. It had a thick, hairy tail upon which it could rest some of its weight when it stood on its hind legs to browse on leaves high up in trees. The Megalonyx, only one of hundreds of kinds of animals that lived in past ages, is a *prehistoric mammal*.

The chart shows the history of life on earth as revealed in the record of the rocks. It shows the eras and periods that are explained on pages 7 and 8 of this book, and it shows the form of life dominant in each phase of the earth's geological history. You can see how late the mammals appeared and how "recently" man emerged.

You know that history means "a record of past events."

**What is the meaning of "prehistoric"?**

Since *pre* means "before," you can see that *prehistoric* means "before a record of past events." More accurately, *prehistoric* means "before a *written* record of past events," because, as we shall learn, events that took place in the far past ages of the earth have left clear and abundant records.

A mammal is a warm-blooded, four-limbed animal that is

**What is a mammal?**

hairy or furry. Mammals are born alive, rather than from eggs, and newborn mammals are nursed on their mother's milk. Dogs, lions, horses, rabbits, seals, elephants, mice, and human beings are examples of mammals.

So, then, prehistoric mammals are warm-blooded, four-limbed, hairy or furry animals that were born alive and were nursed on their mother's milk in the ages before history was written.

The earth is probably five billion years old. In this

**What changes have occurred on the earth in the last five billion years?**

great span of time, the earth has undergone many changes. Scientists believe that during the first half billion years, the earth consisted of molten rock. Sometime between four and four-and-a-half billion years ago, the molten rock cooled enough to form a solid, smooth crust around the earth. Beneath the crust, the rock remained very hot and soft.

In the last four billion years, the crust changed greatly. The smooth rocky surface folded and cracked in many places. Vast blocks of lighter rock, floating on the still-molten rock beneath the crust, formed the earth's continents. Heavier blocks sank, making depressions into which water poured to form the seas that cover three-quarters of the earth's surface.

Time after time, the continual folding of parts of the earth's crust caused mountain chains to rise where the folding took place. Time after time, other

6

Thick clouds surrounded the molten earth for millions of years early in Pre-Cambrian time. Rain from these clouds evaporated as soon as it struck the earth's surface. Later, as the earth slowly cooled, more and more rain remained on earth and ran in streams and rivers to collect in low places where the water formed the first seas and lakes.

**What were the first living things?** About a billion years ago, the first living things appeared on earth. We do not know what they were, but it is a sound guess that each consisted of only a single cell of living matter. The first living things of which we have any record are *algae,* single-celled plants that lived in colonies, much as do the algae of today. (You know algae as seaweed, or as the green or brown slimy growth that you often see on the surface of a pond. And you may find algae as the slippery emerald-green covering on the shady side of trees and rocks.) The earliest animals of which we know are sponges. Also living in the very early period of life on earth were corals and probably jellyfish. All these things lived in the warm seas that covered much of the earth's surface.

**What are the divisions of prehistoric time?** In order to locate events in the very long history of the earth, scientists have divided past time into several units. As you learn about these units, it will help you to understand them if you refer to the chart on pages 4-5. On the left-hand side of the chart you will see four main divisions called *eras.* How have scientists decided what length

ONE-CELLED LIVING MATTER

mountains were formed from lava and ashes spewed forth by volcanoes. And time after time, rain and the running water of streams and rivers wore the mountains down to sea level.

Many times — more than twenty times — the seas overran the continents. Large areas of North America were covered by great shallow seas and vast swamps. Today, farmers ploughing in Kansas sometimes turn up shells from beds of clams that lived 100 million years ago in the sea that covered much of the Middle West.

of time to call an era? There have been times in the past when the earth's crust has experienced very strong and widespread folding that has formed great mountain chains. At the same time, there was an increase in the number of active volcanoes, which also resulted in mountain building. These periods of rapid mountain building are called *revolutions*. The great spans of time between revolutions are *eras*. Since eras are the longest divisions of earth-time, we can call them the volumes in the book of the earth's history.

During each era, smaller foldings of the earth's crust formed mountains and highlands; running water wore the high places down, and the oceans invaded the continents, forming shallow seas; then, the land began to rise again, and the shallow inland seas receded and disappeared. This series of events took place time after time, and each of these series is called a *period*. We may think of periods as the chapters in the volumes of the earth's history.

Each one of the stages within a period — the folding of the crust and the advance and retreat of the seas — marks an *epoch* in the earth's history. Epochs are the pages in the chapters of the earth's history.

There is still another unit of earth-time. It is the *age*, and refers to the kind of living things that dominated a time span. For example, the Age of Hidden Life, the Age of Fishes, the Age of Reptiles, the Age of Mammals, the Coal Age.

**How much is a billion?** As we learn more about the history of life on earth, we shall be talking about millions, hundreds of millions, and billions of years. Let us try to form an idea of what these large numbers mean. Suppose that a boy ten years old were to begin to count at the rate of two every second. And suppose that this boy were to continue to count for eight hours a day — four before lunch and four after lunch, five days a week, and fifty weeks a year. If this boy began to count on a Monday, he would not reach one million until Wednesday morning of the fourth week of his counting. He would have to count for more than seven-and-a-half months to reach

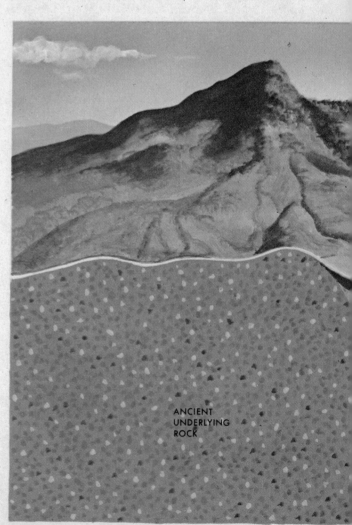

ANCIENT
UNDERLYING
ROCK

10 million. He would be nearly seventeen years old by the time he had counted to 100 million. Before he reached a billion, he would be long past the time when most persons retire from work. He would not count the words "one billion" until the first month of his seventy-seventh year.

When you read about great numbers of years, remember how long it takes someone to count that number at the rate of two every second.

**How is the earth's history recorded?** There are two ways in which prehistoric events have left us a record. The record of what has happened to the crust of the earth is revealed to us in the rocks. The record of past life is revealed by *fossils*, which are the remains of living things of the far past.

There are three kinds of rocks. Those **Igneous rocks** that hardened from molten material, which sometimes rise to the earth's surface from beneath the earth's crust, are called *igneous* (IG-nee-us), or "fire-made," rocks. Quartz is an igneous rock; so are granite and basalt.

Mining tunnels are drilled through different layers of sedimentary rock that were bent by igneous rock pushing up from deep in the earth. Erosion flattened the surface of the land, giving it the appearance depicted by the illustration.

LAYER OF SEDIMENT

SANDSTONE

LIMESTONE

VEIN OF ORE

MINING TUNNEL

Sandstone is a typical sedimentary rock.

Igneous rocks, such as granite (left), form underground when molten rock-matter cools. Other igneous rocks are formed when the molten material comes to the surface as lava.

**Sedimentary rocks**

All kinds of rocks that are on the surface of the earth are eventually worn down and broken into small grains by the action of weather and running water. Streams and rivers carry the rock grains to the lowlands and to the seas. Rock grains that are carried by running water are called *sediment*. Sediment piles up on the lowlands when rivers flood; and it piles up in the sea at the mouths of rivers. Millions of tons of sediment pile up until they cause the solid rock beneath to bend downward. In some places sediment has piled more than ten miles thick. To attain such great thicknesses, the piling-up process had to continue for scores of millions of years.

When grains of sediment are piled to such great thicknesses, the upper layers exert tremendous pressure on the lower layers. This great pressure first squeezes the water from between the grains; then it cements the grains together into solid rock. Rocks formed in this manner are called *sedimentary* (sed-ih-MEN-tary) rocks. Sandstone is a sedimentary rock formed from compressed and cemented sand grains.

Rock grains are not the only source of sedimentary rock. Vast areas of the earth are covered for great depths by the sedimentary rock called limestone. The sediment that forms limestone comes from the breaking and grinding up of coral and the shells of dead shellfish. The grains of this sediment are made of a chalklike material, sometimes called lime. Throughout the hundreds of millions of years since coral animals and shellfish first existed, their pulverized shells have accumulated in vast deposits on the floors of shallow seas. Time and again, the shallow seas have dried up, and the slow, powerful, wrinkling movements of the earth's crust have squeezed the chalky deposits in immense pressure. As a result, the grains of these deposits have been compressed to solid rock. This kind of sedimentary rock is called limestone.

**Metamorphic rocks**

Deep beneath the earth's crust, the rock is very hot and is of a waxy softness. Rock in this condition is called *magma*. In various places, masses of magma slowly push upward into the rocks of the crust. These rocks, when

Metamorphic rocks are formed when heat and pressure change igneous and sedimentary rocks. Marble (left) is changed limestone.

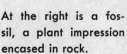
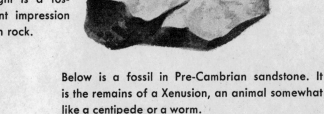

At the right is a fossil, a plant impression encased in rock.

Below is a fossil in Pre-Cambrian sandstone. It is the remains of a Xenusion, an animal somewhat like a centipede or a worm.

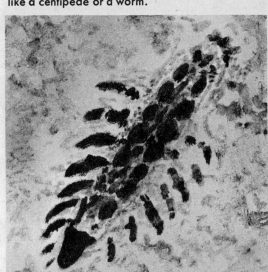

close to the rising magma, are subjected to great heat and pressure, and as a result, they are changed to rocks of a different kind. For example, when a deposit of limestone is invaded by a mass of magma, the limestone is changed to marble. Rocks formed in this manner are called *metamorphic* (met-uh-MOR-fic), or "changed-form," rocks.

**What is a fossil?** A fossil is preserved evidence of prehistoric plant or animal life. Hard parts of animals, such as teeth, bones, and shells have been buried by layers of sediment that later turned to rock. The encasing rock preserved these animal parts from decay. Millions of years afterward, when the rock weathered away, the teeth, bones, and shells could be found in nearly the same condition as when their owners died. Whole skeletons of animals have been found preserved in this way.

Sometimes whole plants or animals have become fossils by being trapped in some substance that preserved them from decay. Amber is one such substance. Amber looks like clear, dark-yellow plastic. Amber is itself a fossil of the sticky yellow pitch that oozes from the bark of pine trees.

Fossils of insects, leaves, and twigs have been found encased in amber. These living things became caught in the sticky pitch on the trunks and limbs of trees, and after a time, were covered completely by the oozing pitch. Long contact with the air hardened the pitch. The trees died, fell, and decayed. The hardened pitch was buried in the earth, and eventually became amber.

Tar and asphalt are other substances that can preserve animal remains from

Prehistoric North American tar pits, like the La Brea Tar Pits of California, were filled with a sticky mixture of soil and petroleum. These pits were often death-traps for animals.

Fossils of insects have been found encased in amber, originally a sticky material oozing from tree trunks.

decay. Thousands of skeletons of animals have been found in tar and asphalt pits. These pits may at one time have been covered by water. Animals drinking this water became stuck in the tar and were unable to pull themselves free. These trapped animals sank beneath the surface of the tar. The tar hardened to asphalt and preserved the animals buried in it. The Rancho La Brea Tar Pits, near Los Angeles, California, are famous for the thousands of beautifully preserved skeletons that have been dug out of them. Horses, mammoths, wolves, saber-toothed cats, and vultures are among the animals that were trapped in these tar pits.

Ice is a third substance that has preserved animal remains. In Alaska and Siberia whole carcasses of mammoths and rhinoceroses have been found in frozen mud. These animals were found entirely as they were when alive. Bones, skin, hair, toenails, internal organs, and even food in the stomachs of these fossil animals were preserved. Frozen fossils

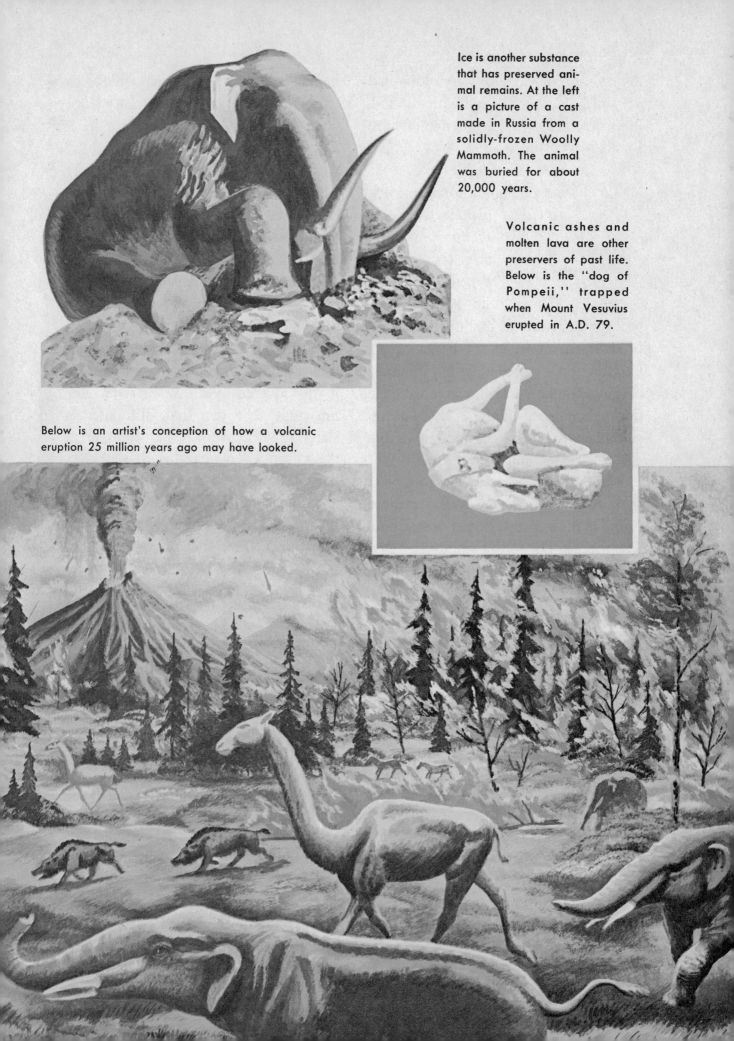

Ice is another substance that has preserved animal remains. At the left is a picture of a cast made in Russia from a solidly-frozen Woolly Mammoth. The animal was buried for about 20,000 years.

Volcanic ashes and molten lava are other preservers of past life. Below is the "dog of Pompeii," trapped when Mount Vesuvius erupted in A.D. 79.

Below is an artist's conception of how a volcanic eruption 25 million years ago may have looked.

are only about 20,000 years old — not very old when compared with the millions of years in which the age of most fossils is measured.

By far the most common fossil-forming process is *petrifaction,* or turning to stone. When sediment is slowly turning to rock, water seeping among the grains of sediment dissolves the bones of the buried animal completely; but minerals dissolved in the water slowly replace the original material of the body. The result is a stone cast, or model, of the skeleton of the animal.

**What is the most common way in which fossils were formed?**

Plants become petrified, too. The most famous petrified fossils are those found in the Petrified Forest of Arizona. The trees of this forest were buried and became petrified. Millions of years later, wind and water uncovered the forest.

Sometimes fossils were formed when ashes from volcanoes covered dead plants and animals. The ashes helped to keep the once-living things from decaying. There are valleys in Oregon and Colorado where such fossils have been found. Poisonous gases from a volcano killed nearby plants and animals. Ashes from the volcano buried the dead. The ashes turned to a kind of rock called tuff, and within the tuff the dead plants and animals became petrified. In Yellowstone National Park there is a cliff that contains seventeen petrified forests, one on top of the other. All the forests are buried in ashes from volcanoes.

Persons who know how rocks and fossils are formed can learn much about the past history of the earth by studying rocks in many parts of the world. Suppose you find a layer of basalt, an igneous rock. On the basalt is a layer of siltstone, a sedimentary rock formed from compressed mud. And on top of the siltstone is a layer of limestone. The layer of basalt tells you that, at one time, molten rock flowed over this area. The siltstone tells you that after the molten rock had cooled, it was covered by a lake or river. The limestone tells you that, still later, a shallow sea covered the same area. Also, you know that the lowest layer had to be formed first, and the layers above formed later, with the uppermost layer last. (Rare exceptions to this rule are found where the folding action of the earth's crust has turned layers of rock completely upside down.)

**What is the record of the rocks?**

Sedimentary rocks can also tell you approximately how long it took for them to be formed. Geologists — scientists who study the earth — have learned how long it takes for a certain thickness-of a particular kind of sedimentary rock to form. For example, it may take 20,000 years to form one foot of a certain kind of rock. Then, if you find a cliff 500 feet high made of this rock, you know it took 10 million years to form.

Rocks reveal a continuous record of life. During the approximately 600 million years since the first living things left their fossil record in the rocks, one kind of plant and animal has succeeded another in an unbroken line of living things. The earth's crust has undergone great changes that have been accompanied by drastic changes in climate and other living conditions. There have been epochs when ice sheets covered much of the earth — hot dry epochs, and mild wet epochs. These changes have brought to an end the existence of thousands of kinds of plants and animals, but *at no time was all life destroyed.*

All these things may be learned by studying the record set forth in the rocks.

# The Succession of Living Things

CAMBRIAN JELLYFISH

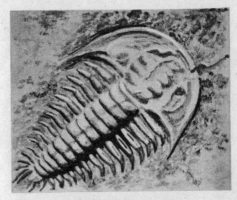

TRILOBITE EMBEDDED IN ROCK

We have learned that the first living things of which we have records were algae, sponges, and possibly some kind of worm. However, in the warm seas of this very early time there were probably many other kinds of living things. The rocks formed at this time are among the deepest sedimentary rocks. They have been broken and covered by igneous rocks many times. So, it is easy to see that, even if most of the living things of this time were not too soft-bodied to form fossils, it still would be difficult to find fossils of them. Because of the lack of fossils, this period of the earth's history has been named the *Cryptozoic Eon* (krip-to-zo-ik EE-on). Cryptozoic means "hidden animal life," and an *eon* is a long period of time of no

**What was the time of hidden life?**

exact length. This time is also called the *Pre-Cambrian* (pree-KAM-bree-un) *Period* for a reason we shall soon learn.

One reason for believing that there were many kinds of living things in the Cryptozoic Eon is that in the rocks above those formed in this eon, we find a great variety of fossils. The animals that formed these fossils must have been developing for millions of years, for they had legs, eyes, mouths, nerves, and muscles. The time during which these fossil-bearing rocks were formed is called the *Cambrian* (KAM-bree-un) *Period*. It began about 520 million years ago and lasted 80 million years.

15

SILURIAN SEA

CAMBRIAN SEA

LOWER DEVONIAN LANDSCAPE

DEVONIAN SEA

In the warm seas that covered much of the earth, there was a great profusion of living things. Chief among them were *trilobites* (TRY-lo-bites), animals that got their names because their bodies were formed in three lobes; that is, they were trilobed. They had feelers protruding from beneath the fore part of their bodies, and they had eyes made up of a great number of lenses — in some trilobites, as many as 30,000 lenses. They had more than twenty legs on each side of their bodies, and they were covered with a horny material like that which covers crabs today. They breathed through gills, as fishes do. The smallest trilobites were less than half an inch long, the longest reached a length of twenty-eight inches, but the average was about one-and-a-half inches. They were carnivorous, which means that they ate other animals.

**What were trilobites?**

Besides trilobites, there were many kinds of sponges and corals in the Cambrian seas. There were clamlike shellfish that were preyed upon by starfish. Small centipede-like creatures crawled on the sea bottom, and jellyfish floated in the water above. A most unusual animal was the *crinoid* that looked just like a graceful plant. It stood on a long stalk that rested on the sea bottom. Of course, the stalk had no roots.

During the next period, the *Ordovician* (or-do-VISH-in) *Period*, also 80 million years long, starfish increased greatly in numbers and kinds. Many types of sea

**What were the first things to live on land?**

snails appeared, some of them giants almost two feet across. Other shellfish with coiled shells lived in the seas. Dominating life in the Ordovician seas were the *nautilids*, animals with long, tapering shells. From the large end of the shell, a head with two eyes protruded. Growing out of the head were as many as ten tentacles, in much the same manner as those of the cuttlefish of today. Nautilids varied in length from half a foot to giants of fifteen feet. Their shells were beautifully colored and marked with intricate designs. Nautilids preyed on trilobites, and as a consequence, the number of trilobites was greatly lessened.

By the end of the Ordovician Period, the first living things appeared on land. They were mosses, much like those we see today.

The 40-million-year period that began 360 million years ago is the *Silurian* (sih-LOO-ree-in) *Period*. All animal life still lived in the seas. The nautilids decreased greatly in number, and those surviving had coiled and frilled shells. Crinoids, many beautifully colored, still waved about on their stalks in response to currents at the bottom of the sea. King crabs appeared, and they have changed but little in all the hundreds of millions of years from the Silurian Period to the present. The first fish appeared, too. There were many kinds, none more than three or four inches long. Some trilobites still crawled on the sea bottom. But the form

**What was the giant animal of the Silurian Period?**

STYLONURUS, THE GIANT SEA SCORPION

of life that dominated this period was the sea scorpion. These sea-living animals looked very much like the scorpions that live on land today. There were many kinds of sea scorpions, varying in length from two-inch pygmies to nine-foot giants.

At the end of the Silurian Period, mosses developed into new kinds of plants. These were merely branching stems, without leaves or roots, not more than eight inches tall. They were soon followed by ferns.

**How did the first soil form?** The period that began 320 million years ago and lasted 55 million years is the *Devonian* (dee-vo-nian) *Period*. This period brought about a dramatic change on the land areas of the world. The mosses and ferns developed into plants of many different kinds and covered the naked rocks of the land with a carpet of green. As the new plants died by the millions, their decaying remains mixed with grains of sediment left by the retreating seas, and the first real soil was formed.

In this soil, ever more abundant plants grew. The soil was able to hold moisture as well as minerals needed by plants. As plants helped to form soil in which to grow, they were able gradually to grow farther and farther away from shore. Ferns developed into tree-like plants, and toward the end of the Devonian Period, some of these had simple leaves. All the many different kinds of plants reproduced by means of spores — just as modern ferns do. The spores were carried by wind and water, and plants sprang up in new locations. However, in order that plants may grow from spores, much water is needed. So, it was only in rainy seasons that spores could develop into plants in inland areas. In Devonian time, the climate was usually mild and wet all over the world.

**When did the fishes develop?** A wide variety of fishes developed and thrived in the Devonian seas. Some were very small, and others were large, such as the first sharks. Some were covered with a thick bony armor, some with small scales, and others had smooth skin. All had fins of some kind to steer and propel them through the water. But most important, these primitive fishes were the first large *vertebrates* — animals with a narrow backbone and skeleton *inside* their body.

In the previous age, the Silurian Period, the *arthropods* dominated the seas. These lobster-like creatures had *external* skeletons. But the arthropods were displaced by the rapid development of the vertebrates during the Devonian Period. These primitive backboned fish became the ancestors of most important animals on land and in the ocean.

The predatory sharks and rays appeared

**When did the first sharks appear?**

during this period. They were powerful swimmers with small eyes and poor vision, and depended on their sense of smell to find their prey. The sharks became one of the most successful animals to evolve. Today there still exist about six hundred living species of sharks in the world's oceans — direct descendants of the sharks that lived 300 million years ago.

One of the largest fishes was *Dinichtys* (din-IK-thees), a name that means "terrible fish." This thirty-foot-long giant had an armored head and powerful jaws with four large bony teeth. The development of a bony jaw released these aquatic animals from their dependence on tiny marine creatures as a source of food. No longer did they have to grub through the mud for their meals — they could now attack and eat any smaller or less aggressive fish. The ocean became a jungle where "big fish eat little fish."

Of equal importance was the development of pairs of bony fins, which ultimately evolved into the arms and legs of terrestrial animals. If fishes with paired fins had not appeared, animals might not have been able to leave the water, and life on land might never have developed.

Some scientists believe that the first animals to move from a life in the sea to a life on land were lung-fishes.

Dinichthys was one of the giants of the early fishes.

The Devonian ancestors of the modern

**What were the first fish like?** fish were the *bony fish,* almost all of which had gills, a skin with scales, and two types of fins: *ray-fins,* supported by dozens of fine, thin bones, and *lobe-fins,* manipulated by a few large bones resembling fingers. Because of their bone structure, the lobe-fins could be twisted so as to give the fish a crawling motion over shallow mud-flats. The lobe-finned fishes also had an inflatable swim-bladder which controlled their buoyancy and which they could use as a lung to live out of the water for brief periods.

The lungfish is a unique modern descen-

**What may have been the first land animal?** dant of the lobe-finned fishes. It has gills that enable it to live under water, as fish do, and lungs that permit it to breathe air, as land animals do. The lungfish probably evolved in stagnant swamps and drying pools where the water held little oxygen. Those lungfish that were able to breathe air at the surface survived. Some developed into the first *amphibians* (am-FIB-ee-uns), a name derived from the Greek *amphi,* meaning "double," and *bios,* meaning "life."

Several species of lungfish still exist today in Australia, South America and Africa. Most are about three feet long, have one or two lungs, and can survive for long periods while buried in mud. If food and water are scarce, an African lungfish will bury itself vertically in moist mud, and build a hard muddy

ERYOPS

In the forests and swamps of the Coal Age, amphibians ran and swam about; giant insects flew in the humid air.

cocoon around itself with a small opening at the top to allow it to breathe through its mouth. In this state it can survive for many months on the fat stored in its own muscle tissue. When it emerges from its muddy cocoon, it quickly gains weight and resumes its normal aquatic life.

Another prehistoric lobe-finned fish that

**What is a coelacanth?** has survived almost unchanged over millions of years is the *coelacanth* (SEAL-a-canth). This "living fossil" was thought to be extinct until 1938, when one was netted by a fishing trawler off South Africa. Paleontologists had unearthed many fossil remains of the

MEGANEURON

bones are hollow, from which comes its name, coelacanth, meaning "hollow spine." Scientists later learned that some African natives had been catching and eating the yellow-eyed fish for many years.

The lungfish and the coelacanth were the ancestors of the amphibians, such as the salamanders, newts, frogs and toads that exist today. In moving from water to land, the early amphibians developed a stronger spine, ears to detect sound in air, tear glands to keep their eyes moist while out of the water, and four limbs to crawl on land. These developments, which represent millions of years of evolution, are reenacted during the brief life of every amphibian.

**How do amphibians reenact evolution?**

The young amphibian grows entirely in the water, breathing through gills and swimming with its tail. As such "tadpoles" grow, they develop limbs, crawl onto land, and breathe through their lungs. But the adult amphibian must return to the water to mate and lay its eggs. The jellied mass of eggs is unprotected and quickly dries up if laid on

coelacanth, but they were astounded to find that the species still existed.

Professor J. B. Smith of Rhodes University, South Africa, saw a sketch of the five-foot-long fish and was able to examine its bones. He recognized it at once as a coelacanth, and offered a large reward for a live specimen. He distributed a leaflet with a photograph of the coelacanth to fishermen along the African coast. Fourteen years later a second specimen was caught, and then six more in 1953 and 1954. To date, about thirty of these fish have been captured.

Unfortunately, the coelacanth does not survive the decompression that accompanies the trip to the surface, and surface water is too warm for it to live. The coelacanth has a large lung, greenish-yellow eyes, and fins that allow it to crawl over the ocean bottom. Its skeletal land. This means that amphibians can never wander far from the water; if the species is to survive, the eggs must be laid and fertilized in water, where they will develop into aquatic larvae.

Many prehistoric amphibians were much larger than their modern descendants, such as frogs and salamanders. The five-foot-long *Eryops* resembled an overgrown tadpole with a wide flat head, short legs, and a short flat tail. It had a scaly, leathery skin and could walk on land. Other amphibians resembled modern crocodiles and spent much of their time in the water. Some developed an armored shell that allowed them to leave the water without dehydrating, and to compete on land with the emerging reptiles. But most prehistoric amphibians probably lived in swamps or ponds and depended upon fish and aquatic life for food. Because of their dependence on the water, amphibians never really conquered the land. They remained a small group within the animal kingdom.

**How was coal formed?**

During the 55 million years of the Devonian Period, there were greater changes than in any other time of equal length in the history of the earth. In the following 55 million years, the coal deposits of North America were formed. Coal is composed almost entirely of the chemical element *carbon*, and for this reason these coal-forming years are called the *Carboniferous* (kar-bon-IF-er-us) *Period,* or the Coal Age.

During the Coal Age, shallow seas flooded North America and much of the land was swampy. The climate was hot and rainy. The plants that had spread over the land during the Devonian Period now became thick forests of tall trees. These trees were not woody, nor did they have bark, as modern trees do. Instead, they were soft and spongy, and their trunks were green.

When these trees died, they fell into the swamps, and sank into the mud. The weight of the fallen trees and the mud pressed heavily on the trees buried beneath. Later, the tremendous pressure of the Earth's folding crust squeezed the buried trees some more, changing them into coal.

In the forests of the Coal Age, many scorpions and spiders crawled among the trees. From these two creatures several kinds of insects developed. Most were more than two inches long, and many exceeded eight inches. Dragonflies with wingspreads of thirty inches preyed on four-inch cockroaches.

**What was the "Age of Reptiles"?**

The first animals to truly dominate the land were the reptiles. About 300 million years ago some amphibians began fertilizing their eggs within the body of the mother. Such internal fertilization was much more reliable than the amphibian method of laying eggs in the water and scattering the sperm nearby. Moreover, the new and improved egg had a leathery shell, so that it did not dehydrate and could be deposited in a hole scraped in the damp earth.

Freed from dependence on water, numerous species of reptiles developed and multiplied. This was the Age of

Reptiles, the *Mesozoic Era,* which spans the period from about 200 to 100 million years ago. Birds, mammals and a variety of insects also evolved during this time, but the reptiles dominated the land.

**Why was the reptilian egg so important?**

The reptilian egg has a large yolk which serves as food for the growing embryo within. The rigid eggshell is porous, so as to allow oxygen to pass through and be absorbed by blood vessels in a membrane called the *chorion,* just beneath the shell. Blood vessels within the chorion transport the oxygen to the developing embryo. A second membrane, the *amnion,* holds the embryo in a protective bag of fluid. Water is supplied by the white of the egg, called the *albumen.* This life-supporting package gives the embryonic reptile enough food and protection to allow it to grow for a long time before hatching. It then emerges from the egg at an advanced stage of development, which gives it a better chance for survival.

Although they laid their eggs on land, the first reptiles stayed close to the water. They fed on fish and amphibians, and some of them resembled crocodiles. Later, *herbivorous* (her-BIV-oh-rus), or plant-eating, reptiles appeared. These animals were much larger because they needed to eat large amounts of plants to gain enough nourishment. Some reptiles developed large, sail-like fins on their backs. By turning the sail toward or away from the sun, the sail would absorb varied heat, and thus the reptile could regulate its own body temperature.

Some reptiles developed sharp teeth and fed upon other reptiles. Some became light-boned and *bipedal,* running on their two hind legs after their prey. Many developed horny, beak-like mouths or duck-bills.

Some reptiles developed a long neck, sharp teeth and a most unusual feature — feathers. The earliest known bird has the scientific name of *Archaeopteryx* (ar-kee-OP-ter-iks), which means "ancient wing." Its fossil was discovered well-preserved in limestone. This bird was about the size of a small pigeon, and had bony claws at the tips of its wings. Perhaps the claws helped it to climb among the trees, and though a bird, it may not have been able to fly. Its jaw was lined with rows of small teeth, a characteristic which indicates to paleontologists that it was a meat-eater.

**What were some of the dinosaurs in the Age of Reptiles?**

The *dinosaurs,* or "terrible lizards," were by far the most outstanding of the reptiles. It was these that grew to great size. The *Brontosaurus* (bron-tuh-SOR-us), or "thunder lizard," was a plant-eater, about seventy feet long and weighing thirty tons. There were a number of dinosaurs with varying numbers of horns that looked like extra-large rhinoceroses. For example, *Triceratops* (try-SER-uh-tops), the "three-horned one," had a head seven feet long, the rear part of which was a frilled bony collar. It had three-foot horns behind its eyes, and a third horn at the front of its beaklike snout.

The most savage dinosaurs were

Toward the end of the Age of Reptiles, some dinosaurs had grown to great height and enormous bulk.

those that walked upright on their three-toed hind feet. These hind feet had long, sharp claws, and were used for walking, holding prey, and fighting enemies. The forelegs were tiny. These fierce dinosaurs had huge jaws and long, sharp teeth backed by powerful jaw and neck muscles. They were feared by all other animals living at the same time. One of these dinosaurs was *Tyrannosaurus Rex* (ty-ran-uh-SOR-us rex), "king of the tyrant lizards." It was more than forty feet long and twenty feet high. The length of one of its steps was fourteen feet.

**Why did the dinosaurs die out?** In a very short time, at the end of the Mesozoic Era, the giant dinosaurs disappeared from the face of the earth after having ruled animal life for about 120 million years. No one knows exactly why. The Mesozoic Era, like the Paleozoic, ended with much mountain-building and a sharply cooler and drier climate. Swamps dried up. Fewer of the thick, spongy marsh plants grew in the cooler climate. The lack of these plants must have taken food from the plant-eating dinosaurs, and they died out. As the plant-eating dinosaurs gradually disappeared, the flesh-eating dinosaurs lost their main source of food. The flesh-eaters, in their turn, died out.

This possible reason for the extinction of the dinosaurs takes on added value when we learn that plant-eating dinosaurs had been fighting a losing battle with the flesh-eating dinosaurs. The plant-eaters had very small brains, which probably means that they were not intelligent animals. The flesh-eaters had larger brains and therefore, greater intelligence. As generation after generation of flesh-eaters became more cunning, swifter, and more terribly armed with great teeth and claws, they became better and better able to hunt and kill the plant-eaters. The flesh-eaters were slowly wiping out their chief source of food, the plant-eaters. When, in addi-

24

PTERODACTYL

TYRANNOSAURUS REX

BRONTOSAURUS

TRICERATOPS

ARCHAEOPTERYX

tion to having to struggle against their flesh-eating enemies, the plant-eating dinosaurs were faced with a lack of food, the plant-eaters' end was hastened. Then, the end of the flesh-eaters came even more rapidly.

It is important to understand that the cooling of the climate was not a change that took place at the end of a summer or even within a year or two. The cooling was gradual, and followed the slow rise of the land during many millions of years. Not even the longest-lived dinosaur nor a dozen generations of

dinosaurs could have noticed a change.

The extinction of dinosaurs may have been further hastened by certain small intelligent animals that appeared toward the end of the Mesozoic Era, and took to feeding on the eggs of large reptiles. These animals were mammals. Dinosaurs, like all reptiles, did not protect their eggs after they laid them and buried them in damp sand. So the eggs would have been easy prey for the little intelligent mammals. Destruction of dinosaur eggs meant, of course, that fewer dinosaur young hatched.

# The Age of Mammals

When the Mesozoic Era came to an end, with mountains rising and temperatures cold and dry, a new era began. The new era was the *Cenozoic* (see-no-zo-ik), or Era of Recent Life. This era began about 60 million years ago and ended only 20,000 years ago. You will remember that the Paleozoic Era lasted 335 million years and the Mesozoic Era 120 million years; so the Cenozoic is by far the shortest of the eras. As you may see from the chart on pages 4-5, the Cenozoic is divided into epochs, as though it were only a period instead of an era.

At the beginning of the Cenozoic Era, mammals were small creatures, few larger than a terrier. Only 15 million years later — a short time in our book of the earth's history — some mammals were gigantic, and all over the world, mammals ruled animal life on land. From that time to the present, mammals have continued to dominate life on land. No wonder that the Cenozoic Era is called the *Age of Mammals*.

While mighty dinosaurs were still ruling the Age of Reptiles, the first mammals were scurrying about the land. And several million years before the appearance of the first mammals, there was a medium-sized reptile, *Cynognathus* (sy-no-NAITH-us), that had some features that mammals were later to have. For this reason, Cynognathus is believed to be a direct ancestor of mammals. Cynognathus, about seven feet long, had teeth somewhat like mammals were to have; the canine teeth were lengthened and the tips of all the other teeth were sharper than the tips of reptiles' teeth. Cynognathus had strong legs and carried its body higher off the ground than reptiles

**What were the first mammals?**

DICINODONT

DICINODONT

CYNOGNATHUS

Several million years before the appearance of the first mammals, mammal-like reptiles such as the Dicinodont, a herb-eater, and Cynognathus, a flesh-eater, roamed south Africa.

do. What is more, its feet, like the feet of mammals, were beneath its body, instead of being extended out from the sides, as the legs of reptiles are. Unfortunately, we have not found the fossil skeletons of the animals that must link Cynognathus to the first true mammals.

Since mammals seem to have developed from reptiles, it is probable that, like reptiles, the first mammals hatched their young from eggs, as the modern duck-billed platypus does. We do not have direct evidence to prove this, but we do know that among the first mammals were *marsupials* (mar-soo-pee-ils), animals that are born alive, but not fully developed. Newborn marsupials live the first part of their lives protected and nursed in a pouch attached to the mother animal. Kangaroos and opossums are present-day marsupials.

You can easily see that a newborn mammal had a **What advantages for survival did mammals have?** much better chance to survive than did a newly-hatched reptile. The newborn mammal was protected and fed by its mother; the newly-hatched reptile had to protect and feed itself. In the cool years that ended the Mesozoic Era, newly-hatched reptiles must have had a difficult time feeding themselves and protecting themselves from cold. As a result, few of the newly-hatched reptiles lived long enough to grow up to become adults. Newborn mammals, fed and warmed by their mothers, began life with a great advantage over young reptiles.

Another advantage mammals had was that of being warm-blooded. This means that the temperature of mammals' bodies remained pretty much the same, no matter what the temperature of their surroundings. On the other hand, reptiles were cold-blooded; their body temperature was about the same as their surroundings. One reason that mammals could keep their body temperature at a constant level is that mammals had fur. This hairy covering kept heat from leaving a mammal's body faster than the mammal could obtain more heat from its food. (Of course, some modern mammals do not have fur, but they have other ways of holding their body heat. For example, human beings wear clothes, and whales and elephants have thick layers of fat beneath their skin.)

In the long, cool period that followed the end of the Mesozoic Era, the great reptiles were sluggish and could not move about very actively, because their body temperature was lowered by the cool air or water in which they lived. Mammals, warmed by their fur, could run about as actively as necessary in order to find food and protection.

A third advantage mammals had was higher intelligence. The first mammals were not very intelligent when compared with modern mammals, but their fossil skulls show that they already had bigger brains than even the flesh-eating reptiles that were then ruling the world. Millions of years later, when the climate became too harsh for most of the reptiles, the mammals, which by now had developed quite large brains, used their intelligence to help them survive. Mammals probably were intelligent enough to migrate southward during the coldest times, thereby finding warmth and green plants upon which to feed. Also, they probably were intelligent enough to hide in caves and to dig burrows to protect themselves and their young from the weather and from hunting reptiles.

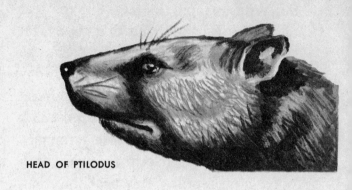

HEAD OF PTILODUS

We have learned that during the first

**What took mammals so long to develop?**

15 million years of the Cenozoic Era, mammals developed from little animals to huge ones. This fact becomes more interesting when we know that mammals had been living for almost 80 million years. In this same length of time, small reptiles had developed into gigantic dinosaurs of many kinds; yet, meanwhile, mammals remained small and insignificant. Why?

The answer, probably, is that the earliest mammals simply could not compete with the well-developed, well-armed reptiles, some of which fed on the little mammals. One of the little mammals that lived during the Age of Reptiles was the *Ptilodus* (TILL-o-dus), which was about the size of a woodchuck. Two other, perhaps smaller, mammals were *Zalambdalestes* (za-lam-da-LESS-teez) and *Ctenacodon* (teen-ACK-o-don). Ptilodus was a plant-eater; the other two were insect-eaters. Little mammals like these, in order to survive, had to keep out of the way of the ruling reptiles. Today, many little mammals are able to live in the Asian jungles by running and hiding from tigers, leopards, and other large meat-eaters. This is probably the way in which early mammals were able to live in the prehistoric jungles at the same time as the dominant reptiles.

When the cold climate at the end of the Mesozoic Era killed off most of the reptiles, the little mammals were rid of their chief enemies, and were free to develop into some of the giants of the animal world.

We learned that marsupials were among

**What are "living fossils"?**

the first mammals. Marsupials appeared more than 100 million years ago, and during almost all of this great length of time, one kind of marsupial, the opossum, has been living. For this reason, opossums are called "living fossils." It is interesting to speculate that during the late Mesozoic Era all mammals were somewhat like the opossum.

Opossums are slow, and do not have large teeth or claws with which to protect themselves against their natural enemies. When an opossum faces danger, it suffers so great a shock that it falls into a deathlike coma. In this state, an opossum can be struck, pinched, poked with sharp objects, and otherwise roughly handled without showing any signs of life. This strange behavior may cause the opossum's attacker to leave it for dead. When danger is past,

HEAD OF ZALAMBDALESTES

The only clues to the early mammals are tiny jaw-bones. The illustration above is very much enlarged.

the opossum revives. This whole performance is called "playing 'possum." Surely, playing 'possum has saved the lives of numberless millions of opossums in the tens of millions of generations since they first appeared. Yet, this one trick does not really explain the puzzle of the opossums' long existence.

A female opossum bears as many as twenty bee-sized young once or twice a year, and is able to nurse about a dozen. Of the newborn opossums, about seven live to become adults. This number of survivors increases the opossum population almost fourfold once or twice a year.

Opossums are able to eat almost anything that is edible; they eat insects,

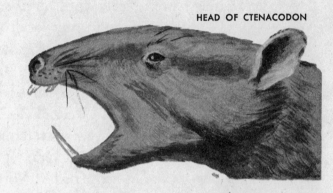
HEAD OF CTENACODON

Taeniolabis, one of the earliest mammals, looked much like a modern woodchuck.

Two "living fossils": the opossum (left), and the platypus (right).

snails, roots, fruits, birds and birds' eggs, lizards, carrion, and garbage.

All during the 90 million years that opossums have existed, the enemies of these unarmed animals have found opossums to be easy prey; yet opossums have survived because the female opossum has raised large numbers of young until they were able to care for themselves and live on almost any food.

There was one time, however, when the opossums' ability to survive must have failed. There are no fossil opossum remains in North America for a period of 30 million years stretching from about 42 to 12 million years ago. No one knows what happened to North American opossums during this long time. Opossums now in North America came from South America.

Modern mammals are not only those that are living today, such as the ones that we see in zoos and circuses. Modern mammals also include those that lived as long as 60 million years ago.

**What are placental mammals?**

The main way in which modern mammals are different from those like the duck-billed platypus or marsupials is that modern mammals give birth to live, fully-developed young. This kind of mammal is called a *placental* (pla-SEN-tl) mammal. Dogs, cats, horses, cows, rabbits, human beings, and nine-tenths of all other mammals living today are placental mammals.

Placental mammals appeared during the Age of Dinosaurs, not very long after marsupial mammals appeared.

These early placental mammals, like the marsupials, have left a "living fossil" from which we can get an idea of what the first placental mammals were like. This "living fossil" is the solenodon that lives in Cuba and the Island of Hispaniola (Haiti and the Dominican Republic). A solenodon is about the size of a small cat. It is as slow and sluggish as an opossum. It has stiff hair on its neck and shoulders, but on its hind quarters are tight tufts of woolly hair, somewhat like soft scales. Its eyesight is poor and so is its hearing. Its head and neck are placed so low and are so heavy that it cannot walk straight ahead, but must sidle like a crab. Like the opossum, the solenodon is defenseless against its enemies. Also, like the opossum, it eats just about anything that an animal can possibly eat. But, unlike the opossum, the solenodon gives birth to only one young at a time. Man now hunts the solenodon for its flesh, and the extinction of this animal is near. But how it managed to survive for more than 60 million years is a mystery.

The solenodon is a "living fossil" of Hispaniola.

30

BARYLAMBDA

CORYPHODON

PANTOLAMBDA

The first 10 million years of the Cenozoic Era is called the **What mammal had a hoof on each toe?** *Paleocene* (PALE-ee-uh-seen) *Epoch,* or Epoch of Ancient Recent Life. About the middle of this epoch, there lived one of the earliest hoofed mammals, the *Pantolambda* (pan-toe-LAM-da). It was about as large as a sheep. It had a long, low skull in which the canine teeth were large, the upper canines protruding along the sides of the lower jaw. Its legs were heavy, its feet rather short, and all the toes were present, each toe having a small hoof. The Pantolambda probably browsed on the leaves of trees.

A few million years later, toward the end of the Paleocene, there lived a descendant of the Pantolambda — the *Barylambda* (bar-ee-LAM-da). This, too, was a many-hoofed animal. It stood more than four feet high — about the height of a pony — and was eight feet long. It was even more heavily built than its ancestor, the Pantolambda. Its hind legs were a little longer than the forelegs, so that the Barylambda was tipped slightly forward. It had a thick, heavy tail, very much like a reptile's tail. Its short, blunt face and teeth probably mean that it grubbed for roots.

Nearly 60 million years ago, a large **Coryphodon** mammal wandered over the flatlands of North America. This animal was the *Coryphodon* (CO-RIFF-o-don), whose name means "pointed tooth." The teeth that gave Coryphodon its name were long, needle-pointed canines in both the upper and lower jaws. In modern mammals, almost all those that have long canine teeth are flesh-eaters, but Coryphodon was a browser; that is, it ate leaves and stems of plants. Its heavy

NOTHARCTUS

about 45 million years ago, but lived on in Asia another 10 million years.

About 50 million years ago, in what is now Wyoming, a little mammal, the *Notharctus* (NO-THARK-tus), ran and climbed about the forests in search of insects and fruits. The name of this little animal means "false bear," because its fossil was first thought to be that of a very small bear. Notharctus was about three feet long, half of which was the length of its tail. This tail probably could be curled about a tree branch in the same manner as a monkey's. Notharctus had a thin, foxlike face, large eyes, and finger-like grasping toes on all its four feet. It resembled a modern lemur, and, in fact, it is the oldest known ancestor of the family to which lemurs and monkeys belong. Compared with other animals of its time, Notharctus probably was very intelligent, because it had a large brain for its size.

**Notharctus**

ZEUGLODON

UINTATHERIUM

body, covered by a nearly-hairless skin, was supported by short, powerful legs and five-toed feet. Each toe ended in a small hoof. This large, slow-moving animal had a thin tail that probably ended in a tuft of hair. Coryphodon had a very small brain, and consequently it was not an intelligent animal when compared with modern mammals. Fossils of Coryphodon are very common in western North America, but the first one was found in England. These animals died out in North America

Living at the same time as Notharctus was a gigantic sea-dwelling mammal, the *Zeuglodon* (ZOO-GLOW-don). This mammal was sixty-five feet long. Of this length, five feet made up the head, ten feet the body, and the remaining fifty feet the tail. It had forty-four large, sharp teeth in its long jaws, and probably lived on large fish. Just behind its head was a pair of short flippers, while at the end of its long tail were flukes, like those of a modern whale. Despite Zeuglodon's great, well-armed jaws and powerful body, it probably met its match in the great sharks that lived in the seas at this time. At least one kind of shark had jaws that were six feet across.

**Zeuglodon**

A small animal about the size of a terrier was the *Tetraclaenodon* (tet-ra-KLINE-o-don). It lived about the same time as the Pantolambda. The Tetra-

**What was the first animal to live in herds?**

claenodon had a doglike head, including large canine teeth, but it was a plant-eater. Descended from the Tetraclaenodon was the *Phenacodus* (fee-NAK-o-dus). This animal, about the size of a sheep, lived in great numbers on plains and sparsely-treed areas. It was probably the first animal to live in herds. It had a long, low skull, and a pointed, overhanging upper lip, like the modern tapir. It had short, heavy legs, and a long, thin tail.

At the same time that Barylambda wandered about the plains of western North America, a larger cousin of Coryphodon wandered in the country that is now the northern Uinta Mountains of Utah. This animal was the *Uintatherium* (yew-in-ta-THEER-ee-um), whose name means "the beast of the Uintas." The Uintatherium was twelve feet long and seven feet tall at the shoulder. It had a heavy rhinoceros-like body, thick legs, and a thin tail with a tuft of hair at its end. The Uintatherium was the largest animal to live during the Paleocene Epoch.

**What was the largest animal of the Paleocene?**

The most striking thing about the Uintatherium was its six-horned skull. It had two horns behind its eyes, two above the eyes, and two near the end of its nose. Just above were two long, sharp canine teeth that protruded downward from its upper jaw outside its mouth. The horns were actually large masses of bone that grew out of the skull and were covered with skin.

PHENACODUS

TETRACLAENODON

Phenacodus, the descendant of Tetraclaenodon, was perhaps the first animal to live in herds. Uintatherium was one of the largest animals of the Paleocene Epoch.

33

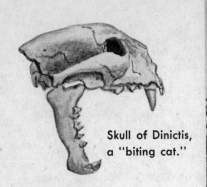

Skull of Dinictis, a "biting cat."

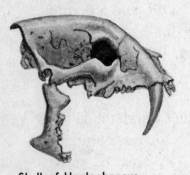

Skull of Hoplophoneus, a "stabbing cat."

SYNDYOCERAS

PATRIOFELIS

MIACIS

The cool climate that began the Paleocene gave way to a warmer climate. By the end of the Paleocene, the climate in North America was warmer than it now is. Figs, magnolias, and other plants that now grow only in tropical or semitropical climates grew as far north as Alaska by the end of the Paleocene. Plants like figs and magnolias are modern plants. So are the plants we call grasses, or grains, such as rye, wheat, oats, and other cereals. So, too, are most flowers, and also hardwood trees, such as oak, maple, walnut, and beech. These plants all have one thing in common: their seeds are covered with tough shells. Such seeds can stand much knocking around without being damaged. They can live through the cold of winter, and then begin to grow when moistened by warm spring

**What kind of plants did plant-eating mammals eat?**

rains. They even can be swallowed by animals without harm. With this wonderful protection, it is not surprising that these seeds spread their plants all over the world. They took the place of the plants that were killed by the late Mesozoic cold. And the spread of these new plants provided food that enabled the browsing and grazing mammals to spread all over the world, too.

About 40 million years ago, small weasel-like animals roamed the forests. From them descended two branches of the cat family. One branch, the biting cats, was represented by *Dinictis* (dy-NICK-tis); the other branch, the stabbing cats, was represented by *Hoplophoneus* (hop-lo-PHON-ee-us). Dinictis means "terrible weasel" and refers to Dinictis's ancestors; Hoplophoneus means "armed slayer." Both

**Dinictis; Hoplophoneus**

DINICTIS

HOPLOPHONEUS

of a modern jaguar; Dinictis was smaller, more slender, and swifter.

One of the animals upon which both Dinictis and Hoplophoneus may have **Syndyoceras** preyed was *Syndyoceras* (sin-dee-o-SAIR-us), a deerlike hoofed animal that lived on the plains of North America. This mammal, about the size of a collie, had four horns. Two, behind the eyes, curved inward and two, near the end of the nose, curved outward and backward. On the end of each of the horns was a small knob. These horns were not antlers like those of a deer, nor were they made of the horny material such as the horns of a cow or a prongbuck. Instead, the horns of Syndyoceras were growths of bone that grew out of its skull, like the horns of a modern giraffe; and probably like those of the giraffe, Syndyoceras's horns were covered with furry skin.

these cats had large upper canine teeth and small lower canines; but the upper canines of Hoplophoneus were twice as long as those of Dinictis. Hoplophoneus used its long canine teeth to stab its prey; Dinictis bit its prey. In order to use its stabbing teeth efficiently, Hoplophoneus had to open its mouth very wide. It was able to open its mouth so wide that the lower jaw pointed straight down. In this position the lower teeth did not interfere with the big upper stabbing teeth. Dinictis, on the other hand, could not open its mouth as wide, but it had a thick lower jawbone much more heavily hinged to the upper jaw. This type of jawbone and hinge mean that Dinictis had powerful cheek muscles to enable it to give death-dealing bites to its prey. Some scientists believe that Dinictis may have been both a biting and stabbing cat. Hoplophoneus was heavily built and was about the size

The beginning of the *Eocene* (EE-o-seen) *Epoch,* that suc-**What was the** ceeded the Paleocene, **first cat?** found mammals well established in a world of mostly mild climate and plentiful vegetation. The name Eocene means "dawn of the recent." It was named before scientists decided to make its earliest part into a separate epoch, the Paleocene. The Eocene began 50 million years ago and lasted 15 million years.

In the forests and fields of the Eocene, the first known cat hunted. It was *Patriofelis* (pat-ree-o-FEEL-is), or "father cat." Patriofelis was as big as

35

a modern lion. Its skull was large, but its brain was not. It had massive jaws that held teeth adapted to slashing and shearing flesh. Its body was covered with coarse thick hair. Its legs were short and its toes widespread. It was not a fast runner, but it may have been a good swimmer because of its wide feet and long, thick tail.

ARSINOITHERIUM

Although Patriofelis is called the father cat, it has no living descendants. The real ancestor of all modern cats — lions, tigers, leopards, cougars, and others — is the small weasel-like animal that we read about as the ancestor of Dinictis and Hoplophoneus. This little mammal, which was also the ancestor of all modern flesh-eating animals, was *Miacis* (MY-ack-is). Its name means "small pointed," and refers to its teeth, the first flesh-cutting teeth among mammals. Miacis was about the size of a large squirrel. It had a large head, large ears, and a long tail. On each foot it had five toes, each bearing a sharp claw. The claws aided Miacis to climb trees and to catch and hold the animals on which it preyed.

The epoch that followed the Eocene was the *Oligocene* (O-LIG-O-seen), and means "little of the recent." During this epoch, which lasted 10 million years, the climate remained mild.

BRONTOTHERIUM

CYNODICTIS

OREODONT

Sioux Indians, hunting bison in South Dakota and Nebraska, now and then found huge bones that had washed out of the earth during heavy rainstorms. Having no idea of extinct animals, the Sioux explained the great bones by believing that they belonged to "thunder horses" that jumped from the sky to the earth during thunderstorms. Once on earth, the thunder horse used its powerful hoofs to kill bison. The huge bones really belonged to *Brontotherium* (bron-tuh-THEER-ee-um). This name means "thunder beast," and was given by a scientist who knew the Sioux legend.

**What were the "thunder horses" of the Indians?**

The Brontotherium was fifteen feet long and stood eight feet high at the shoulder. At the end of its nose, it had a large flat horn made of bone. Although its kind existed for millions of years, they finally died out because they could not develop the type of teeth that were needed for eating the new and tougher grass that grew where Brontotherium lived.

About 35 million years ago, in what is now Egypt, there lived a large mammal, eleven feet long and five-and-a-half feet high at the shoulder. This was the *Arsinoitherium* (ar-SIN-o-ee-THEER-ee-um). It had an elephant-like body and a rhinoceros-like head with four horns. The two horns above the eyes were short knobs, but the two front horns were huge pointed weapons that reached forward over the animal's nose. The horns were so heavy that they needed extra support, which they had in the form of a bar of bone between the nostrils and attached to the upper jawbone. Scientists are not sure to what animals Arsinoitherium may be related. One possible relative is the elephant and another is a little African animal, the hyrax.

In the Badlands of South Dakota, the fossil hunter can find seemingly numberless remains of Oligocene mammals called *Oreodonts* (or-REE-o-donts). There are more Oreodont bones in museums

**What is the most common fossil?**

than those of any other kind of prehistoric animal. There were many kinds of Oreodonts, but all had piglike bodies and most had four-toed feet. We know much about Oreodonts; we even know that, because of a large larynx, an Oreodont must have been able to make a very loud sound. Huge herds of Oreodonts roamed the plains of western North America 35 million years ago.

There lived in South Dakota, at the same time as the Oreodonts, a small foxlike animal, *Cynodictis* (sigh-no-DICK-tis). This name means "dog stabber" and refers to the animal's sharp teeth. This descendant of Miacis was the ancestor of all dogs, bears, raccoons, and weasels. (See page 37.)

The next epoch was the *Miocene* (MY-o-seen), which means "less of the recent." During this epoch, there were alternating warm and cool periods. About 25 million years ago, in North America, there lived a mammal whose bones puzzled scientists for quite a time. This animal was *Moropus* (MORE-o-pus), whose name means "foolish-footed." Moropus was a riddle for many years, because its upper body and its feet were believed to belong to two different animals. The upper bones seemed to place Moropus among the odd-toed hoofed animals, but, instead of hoofs, the bones of the feet had large claws. It was not until a whole skeleton of Moropus was found that it was understood that the clawed feet belonged to the upper bones. Some scientists believe that Moropus used its claws to dig

**What was the "foolish-footed" mammal?**

for roots; others believe the claws were used to pull down tree branches while Moropus stood on its hind legs and browsed. (See pages 40-41.)

Another Miocene mammal was *Dinohyus* (dy-no-HY-us), a hog that stood six feet tall at the shoulder, and was eleven feet long. Its skull was almost a yard long, and its upper canine teeth protruded along the side of its mouth as two sharp tusks. (See pages 40-41.)

About five million years after Cynodictis lived, one of its descendants hunted in the western part of North America. This was *Daphoenodon* (daf-EEN-o-don), whose name means "bloody tooth." It was about four-and-a-half feet in length. Its long, low-slung body, long tail, and short powerful legs were catlike, but it had a long wolflike head. Daphoenodon was the ancestor of modern bears and dogs. Perhaps one of the animals that Daphoenodon hunted was *Ilingoceros* (il-ling-o-SAIR-us), a pronghorn antelope with two spiraled horns. Another animal Daphoenodon may have hunted was *Prosynthetoceras* (pro-sin-thet-o-SAIR-us), a deerlike hoofed mammal. It had two forward-curving horns between its ears and a single branching horn at the end of its nose. (See pages 40-41.)

**What animal was the ancestor of modern bears and dogs?**

About 10 million years ago, the *Pliocene* (PLY-oh-seen) *Epoch* began, and with it came a gradual cooling, as the folding of the earth's

**What animal was the largest of the stabbing cats?**

crust raised the continents high and glaciers began to move down from the north. Pliocene means "more of the recent." It was during the Pliocene that the stabbing cats grew to be largest and fiercest. The largest of these was *Smilodon* (SMY-low-don), or "carving-knife tooth." Smilodon is usually called a saber-toothed tiger, but tigers are biting cats that belong to the other branch of the prehistoric cat family. Smilodon was shorter than a modern lion, but it was more heavily built. Protruding from Smilodon's upper jaw were thick, pointed, nine-inch canine teeth. This stabbing cat had extremely powerful legs and muscular shoulders that enabled it to cling to its prey while the great saber-teeth slashed and stabbed. Smilodon's nostrils were located a little back from the end of its muzzle, so that this cat could breathe with its nose buried in the thick fur of its victims. How Smilodon chewed its food without its great stabbing teeth being in the way is an unsolved mystery.

Almost all mammals grew to their largest size during the Pliocene. One of these giants was *Castoroides* (kass-tuh-ROY-deez), a beaver ten feet long, including a three-foot tail. These beavers probably could gnaw down the largest tree with ease. (See pages 40-41.)

Many years ago scientists discovered large numbers of fossilized mud corkscrews, reaching about five feet below the surface of the earth. At first, they thought the mud had filled the space left by spiral roots of a plant that had rotted away. Later,

**What was a "devil's corkscrew"?**

it was learned that these regular, evenly-spiraled tubes, nicknamed "devil's cork-screws," were the main entrances to burrows of a mammal called *Cerato-gaulus* (sair-a-tuh-GAWL-us), or "horned digger." This animal, about two feet long, was a rodent that had two sharp horns sticking up from the middle of its forehead. No one is sure how the horns were used. (See pages 40-41.)

All during the Cenozoic Period, there was a wide land bridge between North America and Asia across what is now the Bering Strait. Animals wandered freely back and forth between the two continents. But almost all during this time, until the late Pliocene Epoch, North America was cut off from South America. During the time that a land bridge existed by way of Central America, most of South America was under the sea. However, during the Pliocene, both Central and most of South America were above water so that animals could wander between North and South America.

**Why were South American mammals different from North American ones?**

While South America was cut off from North America, many strange mammals developed on the southern continent. For instance, there was *Bor-hyaena* (bore-hy-EEN-a), a marsupial carnivore that looked much like a giant wolverine. Another marsupial carnivore was *Thylacosmilus* (thy-lack-os-MY-lus), a stabbing cat whose great fangs were protected by a flange of bone that jutted downward from the lower jaw. Also, there was *Toxodont* (TOX-o-

Moropus, the "foolish-footed" mammal.

Dinohyus stood six feet tall at the shoulder.

Daphoenodon, ancestor of modern bears and dogs.

Prosynthetoceras was a deerlike hoofed mammal.

Ceratogaulus was a two-foot long rodent with horns.

Casteroides was a beaver ten feet long, including a three-foot tail.

Smilodon, a saber-tooth cat, was a ferocious animal.

BORHYAENA

MACRAUCHENIA

GLYPTODONT

THYLACOSMILUS

HEAD OF TOXODONT

While South America was cut off from North America, many mammals developed on the southern continent.

dont), a heavy, clumsy, ten-foot-long plant-eater. The *Macrauchenia* (mack-raw-KEEN-ya) had a camel-like body, a long neck, and a short elephant-like trunk. One of the strangest of all the mammals to originate in South America was the *Glyptodont* (GLIP-toe-dont), an armored mammal. The largest of these mammals were fourteen feet long and five-and-one-half feet high. On the end of its tail was a spiked, clublike growth that may have been used as a weapon.

By the end of the Pliocene Epoch, North American mammals were drifting through Central America to South America. Among these animals were carnivores like Smilodon. These flesh-eaters eventually wiped out most of the mammals they found in South America.

About 10 million years ago, there lived in what are now the **Teleoceros** Plains States of North America a rhinoceros called *Teleo-*

*ceros* (tel-ee-o-SAIR-us). The name of this animal means "end horn," and it was so-named because Teleoceros had a horn on the end of its nose. This horn was simply a short knob, quite different from the long horns of the rhinoceroses living in Africa and India today. Teleoceros had short legs that hardly held its long, heavy body off the ground.

**When did the last of the prehistoric mammals die out?** Only a million years ago, the last Cenozoic epoch, the *Pleistocene* (PLICE-toe-seen) began. Pleistocene means "most of the recent." During this epoch the glaciers of the Northern Hemisphere reached their greatest southward advance. In all except the tropical regions, the climate was cold. Four times the ice advanced, and four times it retreated. The last retreat began only 12,000 years ago, and is still going on. During the Pleistocene, the last of the truly prehistoric types of mammals died out. For instance, at the beginning of the Pleistocene, there lived in both North and South America a giant ground sloth called *Megatherium* (meg-a-THEER-ee-um), or "great beast." It was as large as an elephant, and could rear up eighteen feet from the ground to browse on the leaves of trees. About 10,000 years ago, the last of these giants died. Smilodon and Megatherium both died out, the last of the Smilodons living until 8,000 years ago.

**What is the most intelligent and most dangerous mammal of all?** By the middle of the Pleistocene Epoch, there roamed over the forests and plains of the world the most intelligent and most dangerous mammal of all — Man. Man was

Teleoceros was an early rhinoceros that lived about ten million years ago.

The Megatherium was as large as an elephant and could rear up eighteen feet from the ground.

In Europe and North America, there lived a giant deer, Megaceros, which means "great horn." Megaceros is usually called the Irish elk. It had antlers with a spread of twelve feet.

not afraid to attack any of the giant Pleistocene mammals, and there was none that he could not kill. The large brain that enabled mammals to dominate all other land animals has enabled man to dominate all the animals of the world. Man has been able not only to dominate other animals, but also to build his civilizations for two reasons. Man is probably the only animal that can think about things that are not directly connected to objects around him — that is, man can have and use ideas. Secondly, man's hands enable him to hold things and use them in a way no other animal can. (Of course, a monkey has hands to hold things, but a monkey does not have the brains to use such things in the way man can.)

**What was the largest land mammal?** The history of the rhinoceroses is one of many kinds, beginning with *Hyracodon* (hy-RACK-o-don), a very active, hornless rhinoceros that lived during Oligocene times. It looked more like a wild donkey than a rhinoceros. From Hyracodon descended a long line of many kinds of rhinoceroses, some without horns, and some, like those now living in Africa, with one or two long, sharp, scimitar-like horns. We have already met two prehistoric rhinoceroses: Teleoceros and the woolly rhinoceros. The largest rhinoceros — and the largest land mammal ever to live — was the hornless *Baluchitherium* (ba-loo-chih-THEER-ee-um). It was eighteen feet tall at the shoulder, and its head reached three or four feet higher. It could have looked over the roof of a two-story house. The first fossil of Baluchitherium was found in Baluchistan, in 1924.

There were Pleistocene bison, or buffalo, much like the modern bison that once roamed the American western plains in such great numbers. But Pleistocene bison had great horns that extended almost three feet on either side of the head.

HEAD OF BALUCHITHERIUM

In Europe there was a huge rhinoceros fourteen to sixteen feet long. It was covered with a coat of long, heavy hair that enabled it to live in the snows of the Ice Age. This was the Woolly Rhinoceros.

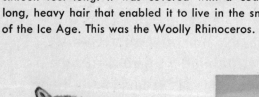

HEAD OF HYRACODON

HEAD OF AFRICAN
WHITE RHINO OF TODAY

WOOLLY RHINOCEROS

Now that we know what kinds of mammals lived in each of the epochs of the Cenozoic Period, let us see how some well-known modern mammals developed through the 60 million years of this period of history.

**How did horses develop?**

Early in the Eocene, running about the plains and glades of North America was a small animal not much bigger than a cat. It had an arched back, four toes on each forefoot and three on each hindfoot. This little animal was *Eohippus* (EO-HIP-us), or "dawn horse." Its toed feet fitted it to run on soft and marshy ground. Eohippus had a bony tail with bristly hairs at its end. Eohippus's teeth were fitted for browsing from bushes. Before the end of the Eocene, Eohippus had been succeeded by two other kinds of horse; one, *Epihippus,* was about the size of a sheep.

During the Oligocene there lived *Mesohippus* (mes-o-HIP-us), or "middle horse." It had only three toes on each foot. This middle toe was the beginning of a hoof.

In the Miocene, there appeared *Merychippus* (mer-ee-CHIP-us), or "grazing horse," a horse about the size of a donkey. Its middle toe had developed into a hoof, while the other toes hung useless at the side of its leg. Hoofs enabled Merychippus to run very fast. Merychippus had the kind of teeth that tell us it grazed on grass.

By the end of the Pliocene there lived in North America the first real horse, *Equus* (EE-kwuss), not very different from the horses we see today.

**What is the development of the camel?**

The first camel was *Protylopus* (pro-TILL-o-pus). It lived during the Eocene Epoch; it was as small as Eohippus (no bigger than a cat), had short limbs, and four-toed feet. During the Oligocene, camels were a little bigger than Protylopus, but they looked very much like their ancestor. In the next epoch, the Miocene, a big, long-legged, long-necked camel, *Oxydactylus* (ox-ee-DACK-till-us), grazed on the plains of North America. Grazing along with Oxydactylus were great herds of a smaller camel, *Stenomylus* (steen-o-MY-lus). It was about the size of a setter and was a very fast runner; for this reason Stenomylus is sometimes called the "gazelle camel." In the Pliocene, wandering the plains of Colorado, was a camel eighteen feet tall. This was *Alticamelus* (al-tee-cam-MEEL-us), or "high camel." Half this height was the animal's long neck. Because of its neck,

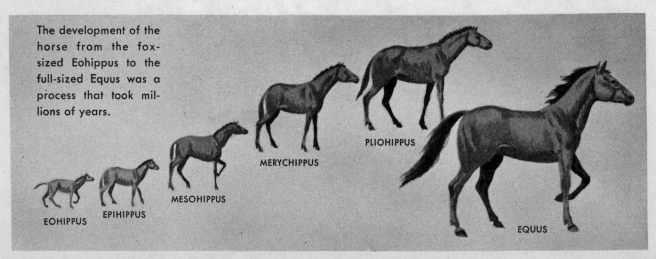

The development of the horse from the fox-sized Eohippus to the full-sized Equus was a process that took millions of years.

EOHIPPUS

EPIHIPPUS

MESOHIPPUS

MERYCHIPPUS

PLIOHIPPUS

EQUUS

It took millions of years for the "modern" camel to evolve, but you can see some of its typical features in the Miocene ancestors.

PROTYLOPUS

STENOMYLUS

ALTICAMELUS

MODERN BACTRIAN CAMEL

Alticamelus is sometimes called the "giraffe camel."

In the Eocene Epoch, a small, blunt-nosed mammal lived in the forest. This was the *Moeritherium* (mee-ree-THEER-ee-um). It was about three feet high at the shoulder, and about as large as a modern tapir. This little animal was the ancestor of all the elephants and elephant-like mammals in the world. A Miocene descendant of Moeritherium was *Trilophodon* (try-LOF-o-don). It

**What was the ancestor of all elephants?**

was ten feet tall and about two feet longer than Moeritherium; this is the size of a large modern elephant. Trilophodon had a trunk and tusks as big as those of a modern elephant, but the remarkable thing about this mammal was its lower jaw, which, with two protruding, tusklike teeth, extended out as far as the trunk could reach — in some species, nearly seven feet. Another Miocene elephant-like mammal was *Dinotherium* (dy-no-THEER-ee-um), twelve feet high at the shoulder, and a resident of Asia and Africa. It had a short trunk and tusks that curved downward.

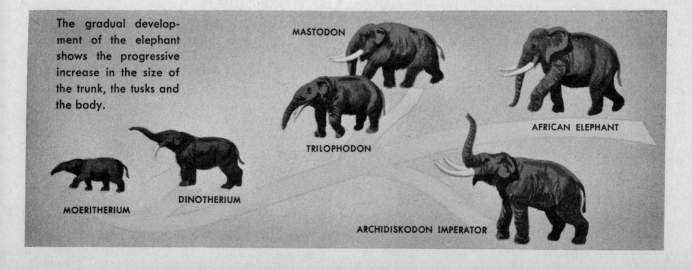

The gradual development of the elephant shows the progressive increase in the size of the trunk, the tusks and the body.

MASTODON

TRILOPHODON

AFRICAN ELEPHANT

MOERITHERIUM

DINOTHERIUM

ARCHIDISKODON IMPERATOR

The line of descent to which Trilophodon and Dinotherium belonged ended in the Pliocene; but another branch gave rise to the *mammoths* of Pleistocene time. These animals had huge, curving tusks, larger than those of any modern elephant. Some of the mammoths that lived in Asia, Africa, Europe, and North America were hairless; others in Europe and Siberia were covered with thick, woolly hair, and are called woolly mammoths. Still another prehistoric elephant-like mammal was the *mastodon* (MAS-tuh-don). This animal dwelled in the forests of eastern North America. It was a huge, shaggy beast with great incurving tusks. It fed on twigs from the evergreen forests that grew widely as the last glacier retreated in North America.

## You and Fossils

We have seen that the fossil record reveals how life began in the sea as a single cell. Then, through a vast length of time, one kind of living thing followed another, in a great variety of sizes and shapes. Some of the earliest kinds of living things — algae, sponges, snails, dragonflies, cockroaches, for example — have survived. Most prehistoric life died out.

The fossil record has shown how strange kinds of mammals have had their turns at dominating land animals, and then have died out. Finally, man has come to dominate all living things. Man, with his spears, arrows, traps, and guns, is on his way not only to dominating all other living things, but to exterminating them.

The record of the rocks is far from complete. We have only a single fossil skeleton, or only a fossil bone or two of many prehistoric animals. In some cases, we have even less. You remember that the first amphibian is known only from a single footprint.

As a result, many pages in the book of prehistoric life remain to be filled in. Many problems remain to be solved. One of the reasons that we do not know why the dinosaurs died out may be that the end of the Mesozoic Era is a time that has not yet been very completely studied. Perhaps you would be interested in trying to fill in the missing pages and solve the remaining puzzles of prehistoric life.

Scientists who study prehistoric life are called *paleontologists* (pay-leon-TOL-o-jists). They study geology, so that they are familiar with the rocks of the world. They study zoology, so that they are familiar with the many kinds of animals. They study paleontology to learn about fossils.

Some paleontologists work outdoors, digging, and carefully crating fossils to be shipped to museums and universities. Then they are mounted, labeled, and studied by other paleontologists. Many paleontologists work both outdoors and in museums. Would you care for this kind of work? There are opportunities for you in this field of science.